**Praise for Nicca Ray's RAY BY RAY from Three Rooms Press**

"*Ray by Ray: A Daughter's Take on the Legend of Nicholas Ray*" is a decade-plus project that tells all in a way that's true to [author Nicca Ray] and true to her father…an intimate first-hand grasp on the benefits and hindrances of drugs and alcohol – along with front-row access to the Hollywood scene …In *Ray by Ray*, Nicca stays out of … film talk, rather opening up her own family history to reveal her dad's emotional and professional disintegration, his own twisted-up storylines."

– *Please Kill Me*

"In this intimate blend of memoir and biography, [Nicholas Ray's] daughter, Nicca, a filmmaker and writer, explores her father's complex life and artistic legacy as well as their own complicated relationship and his impact on her life … This contemplative, deeply personal portrait of both Rays will appeal to readers interested in mid-century Hollywood."

– *Library Journal*

"[*Ray by Ray*] is the screamingly sad, wise, drug-fueled, hilarious tale of a daughter's coming to light from under an immense paternal shadow. A deep dark shadow, by mortal standards, a shadow's shadow; for Nick Ray is himself a burnt-out case, an artist swallowed whole by the bottle, the spoon and the syringe."

– *Amos Poe, director, The Blank Generation*

"Nicholas Ray invented the meme of teenage anguish. His daughter Nicca lived it. The first miracle is that she survived. The second is that she created this beautiful, heartbreaking book, in which she maps the intersecting arcs of her life and her father's, creating a dazzling geometry of self-creation and self-destruction."

*– Peter Trachtenberg, author of*
*7 Tattoos and Another Insane Devotion*

# BACK SEAT BABY

ALSO AVAILABLE FROM POISON FANG BOOKS

BY m. c. nuto

Fiction
*You Used to Know Me*

BY CHRIS D.

FICTION
*No Evil Star*
*Dragon Wheel Splendor and Other Love Stories of Violence and Dread*
*Shallow Water*
*Mother's Worry*
*Volcano Girls*
*Tightrope on Fire*

NON-FICTION
*Gun and Sword: An Encyclopedia of Japanese Gangster Films, 1955–1980*

# BACK SEAT BABY

**Poems by Nicca Ray**

**Drawings by Jesse McCloskey**

**Foreword by Ann Magnuson**

**Preface by Chris D.**

**A Poison Fang Book**

***If you enjoy this book, tell someone about it***

A Poison Fang Book



Front and back cover designs by C. D.

ISBN:9798550407714

First Poison Fang Books Edition, November 2020

Printed in the United States

10 9 8 7 6 5 4 3 2 1

***for***
***Barbara Hroza,***
***my forever pea in a very odd pod***

# Preface

Hopefully without my putting too pretentious a point on it, Nicca Ray's writing shows a grace indicative of balance. Not just your ordinary 'I-can-stand-on-one-foot-for-five-minutes' kind of balance, but a cosmic balance...the type of balance one achieves when simultaneously afflicted with an euphoria as well as a nauseating vertigo while perched on the crumbling precipice staring into the abyss.

The grace, the balance, comes from an unconscious unconditional love that would seem exceptional. And perhaps it is, because so few in our world – at least in the public eye – seem to possess it. Where does one get this grace? From an agnostic point of view, I do not believe it comes from an anthropomorphic God, but a small 'g' god, the positive light and invisible strength that radiates outward all around us to empower others as well as one's self, to act as a conduit. To do that, one must relinquish fear and open up to being that conduit, a reservoir for that love. It doesn't shy away from the darkness, but confronts it, pulls its covers off and exposes it to the world, leeches out the poison, so it shrivels into nothingness like a vampire in sunlight.

Some people write to simply, unpretentiously, tell stories. Perhaps they achieve that grace, perhaps they do not. You cannot push it like a product for consumption. Intentionally trying to be a conduit for that grace, to force it, portray it as an aspirational thing – even a commodity – is the worst thing a writer can do. Because it kills its guileless spontaneity and purity of vision. Nicca does not have to ever worry about that. Her survival from childhood, her acceptance of the pain and her resulting grace has enabled her to achieve a transcendence of the all-too-ordinary monstrousness of everyday life. She shows it in her poetry.

*– Chris D.*
*Highland Park, Los Angeles*
*July, 2020*

# Foreword

*"Almost nowhere has my life ever been harder than here in this mausoleum of easy-going. The house is too pretty, and here my profession is gold-digging, the lucky ones pan big nuggets the size of your fist out of the mud and people talk about them for a while; when I walk, I walk on clouds like a polio victim."* – Bertolt Brecht, 1941

I first read Brecht's diary when I was in my impressionable and still optimistic twenties. I had just come to Los Angeles, and his description captured perfectly the fantasyland of Tinseltown. I myself hoped to pan big nuggets of gold, but I was in no hurry – the perpetual sunshine was gold enough. And if a polio victim could walk on clouds, I could do back flips.

Decades – and many ups and downs later – I see Brecht's quote in a different light. Perhaps he meant that the polio victim, who has enough difficulty walking on land, would be doomed to Sisyphean frustration trying to walk on those constantly morphing, tissue-thin clouds.

But, after reading Nicca Ray's book of poems set in LA, both interpretations ring true.

Brecht saw LA as an outsider; Ray is home-grown and so she knows intimately its nooks and crannies, many of its detours. Different generation, same town. Same contradictions.

Ray captures this dichotomy in her poetic Polaroids – snapshots poised between carefree and dread, promises and lies, car crashes and swimming pools – where alienation occupies the same space as the "warm tone cinematography" of 1970s moviemaking.

Hers was a childhood that alternated between sunny beaches and dark secrets, with the dark secrets eventually eclipsing the sun. In "Living in a Thru–Way" she writes "life is emotional paralysis," and the apartment she finds herself in is "this low hung stucco entrapment" with a window "never designed to be open onto....an Avenue meant for traveling through/Not to be a Destination."

You don't have to grow up here to find Ray's poetic odyssey so familiar. Hollywood is part of our DNA, inextricably bound up with our own personal histories and traumas – parental neglect, divorce, alcoholism, addiction. Ray's Jungian road map shows us life in a city that is not so much Dream Factory as fast food drive-thru.

Plumbing the depths of uncertainty and loneliness, Ray finds gold in the collective swamplands of our souls. She nails that "feeling weird" feeling that had a lot of us gravitating towards like-minded misfits, all desperate to find solace within the Tribe of Cool.

Nicholas Ray's rebel was famously without a cause. Nicca Ray's rebel has one: to wake up from the recurring nightmare and change the narrative; to write her way out of the mausoleum; to walk, resurrected, with ease on the streets below as well as the clouds above.

*– Ann Magnuson,*
*Silver Lake, Los Angeles*
*July, 2020*

# Introduction

*Back Seat Baby* is my ode to Los Angeles, to Hollywood, the city I grew up in, the town that bares my battle scars. It is the place I left but can never leave. LA owns my heart, and yet it is a dangerous place for me. I cannot rest nor find peace of mind on her streets. She is a warning sign, a splash of cold water, a wildfire, a longing, a missed golden opportunity, the house where my oldest and dearest friends live, the half of me, the whole of me, the sum of my parts.

*Nicca Ray,*
*New York City, NY*
*July, 2020*

## PINATA

Seatbelts aren't the law yet brake for the red light the sudden stop sign the last sun ray hitting the lone palm tree the cross where Jesus died on the distant mountain top the exodus the parking space across the street from the open marketplaces she says remind her of when we lived in Madrid. I don't remember cobblestone or slabs of meat hanging from racks or baskets and flowers or Terra Verra pottery but I remember the pinatas she hung from the shady tree in our backyard just east of Hollywood and on my birthday hitting the blue, purple, yellow and orange papier mâché horse with a baseball bat and opening my eyes just a slight crack so I could see where all the candy fell.

## LOVE-IN

Under the Oak-Walnut Woodlands
Jeweled horses ride the carousel
A parade of longhair flower children grown-ups go forth
Patchouli baths
No need for mud pies
They pass around whiskey flasks and
Vats of crystal clear persuasion
Drumming beats for drumbeat dancers
She dances the magnetic field
Her flowing arm gestures
The seascape
A wave curling
Whitewash rolling in
The drumbeat

## BACK SEAT BABY

The barefoot smears yellow guash across
the full moon hangs
over the hill
miles from the French windows my best friend and I look
out of
Frightened by the monster we're certain will crash through
the glass if we don't lock up
tight and cover with the white sheets my mother uses to lay
out across the sandy beaches
Ruffles with ridges tuna fish sandwiches sunny days.

In memory I trick myself with tales of having lived in a
haunted house
The man and boy who did bad things were born that way
It was no Amityville Horror.

In the afternoon when the sky is clear there are five palm
trees in the distance I think are
Hawaii
If only we could fly there in the dark
Escaping to paradise.

Tiptoe down spiral staircase
coat closets stifle fear
eat a cookie
my sister she runs from man's murderous threats
disappearing for days
while his son
breathes through my heating vent.

In the back seat of my mother's four-door Volkswagen
his son throws a patterned towel over my lap to hide
his roaming hand. In the back seat of the Immanuel
Presbyterian Church bus I let my best friend's boyfriend
feel me up.

Heads go under
ocean whitewash
cleansing
Christians baptize my best friend rises reborn
I am praising Jesus
is no savior
footprint stains me yellow.

## HIDEAWAY

Hedges
Hedging bets
Will he or won't he
Come to my bed tonight
Will she or won't she
Succumb to his leering
Will I or won't I
Be able to sleep tonight
Will she or won't she
Drive the getaway car
Won't he just die
Why can't he just die
Will I or Won't I
Go to hell for these thoughts
Hedges
Blocking driveways
Hedging
Conversations
There's a hedge growing between the garage and our neighbor's cement wall
I hide inside
Hedges
Hedging bets
Am I safe here
Can I live here
Is there food here
Comfort and warmth
Will the sunshine expose the hole
Will the moonlight summon fear
Will I remain silent
Ten more years

## THE POETRY of MOTHER

These men my mother marries they put their hands on my sister beat her to a pulp. Still, my mother disappears with them behind closed doors. She slathers herself with oils, lights scented candles, and lets them slip it in. My sister and I huddle under our blankets and listen to her making the same noise our cat makes when she's in heat. In the morning my sister is gone, and I am left wondering where the poetry is.

*A Little Lipstick*

# BODIES ARE CAGES WE TRAP OURSELVES IN

My mother's mother uses an ice pick to zip her dress
Her knuckles to push quarters across dimestore counters
Ovens to burn Biscotti
Pillows to prop her head
Television to shut off the sounds in her head
Canary yellow nightgowns to spend her days
Vodka to drown her rage
At her daughter's ballerina grace
My mother's elegance amplifies the curse of her mother's crippled hands
And I am a body growing numb
Resting my head on grandmother's belly
Her fleshy mountain of peace
Cradling my thoughts to sleep
Until my mother wakes me
Cigarette in her mouth
She's pointing at the ash dropping off my grandmother's lip to the floor
Accusations roar
My grandmother now a firestarter born
And my mother has come to rescue me from going up in her mother's flames
I would rather burn in my grandmother's hell than drive back up that hill
To the house
Where the teenage boy and his father steal bodies
Body snatchers one and all
As a girl my grandmother defied her God-fearing mother
"Art is the devil's work."

She hid drawings behind baseboards, under bibles
Concealed desires atop stairs
Until lightning struck pastel
Curled her fingers into palms
The sudden illness stealing dreams
I spend nights by my grandmother's side
Sitting for portraits
Watching her direct pencil with knuckle
Faint lines appear on sketch paper
Wisps of hair blow freedom
From ash dropping on the carpet beside my grandmother's bed
The smoke circling my mother's face
The trouble my mother's perfect body bore
A father who took liberties
The husband screaming obscenities
The bed I lay in, stiffly
As if to breathe would kill me

## MOTHER SEX BEAT

Pop drink snort
Windows rattle
Mother moans
Block her out
Pop drink snort
Block her out
Pop drink snort
Block her out
Pop drink snort
Lose mind

## MY FIRST DRUNK

I've got *American Graffiti* in my head cruising Van Nuys Boulevard I'm thirteen-years-old Schlitz Malt Liquor in tall blue cans in the back seat of my older sister's boyfriend's metallic blue Volkswagen Bug. I'm MacKenzie Phillips, the younger sister of the high school beauty queen. If I could just not be my age, I could jump out of this back seat into another and forget I'll never be the girl who's spoken for. If I could be the actress jumping from one part to the next. Living inside a television screen with Richie and Fonzie and *Happy Days* instead of holding a blanket over my head waiting for the yelling to stop, the silence to break, to be old enough, to be brave enough to run away. Revving engines wake me from a momentary drunken slumber. My neck is a giraffe stretching up up up the palm tree trunk toward the moon. A pompom in its midst. My sister cheering on the Varsity quarterback to touchdown. His metallic blue Volkswagen Bug pulls into the parking lot of Farrells, the Gold Rush saloon of Ice Cream Palaces. This is no gunslinging scene out of *High Noon* or pick up at Mel's Drive-In. This is my sister's quarterback boyfriend swinging door open, watching me fall on pavement.

## A SUNNY DAY BIRTHDAY

I was riding in the car with you on that sunny late
afternoon Sepulveda Boulevard the long stretch to the
Valley a yawn traffic light glow

I caught a whiff of your distillery when you kissed my
cheek
That kiss a popping balloon on the not even evening of my
fourteenth birthday

Inside the glove compartment the pint half gone
I still thought mothers knew the dangers of drunk driving
so I reprimanded you
You floored the gas
We became the drive became the swervy celebration

There was nowhere for me
There was no other mother
No other home
There was no one for me to jump out of the car for
Nowhere to get to
I was too far from
A home

***

You'd stopped talking to me
Barely saying hello
For months it had been like this
Do you remember?
I didn't know how to reach you
I'd lost you

Years before
When I failed to break down your bedroom door and pull him off of you
I knew it was too late
You were gone to me
I saw it in your eyes
You cancelled me out
Stared blankly when I spoke
Refused to acknowledge my saying, “I love you”
There was such fury in your eyes
That afternoon of our swervy celebration I wanted you to have
The shoes, the glue, the father, the sun, the moon
A thousand hearts
I had no father to give you
No hand that could turn back time
The afternoon of your fourteenth birthday was a sunny day
The glare was blinding

*Graveyard Oasis*

## MOTHER

She is:
The curtain rising
An everlasting performance
Spoken in Grand Jete

The brush against my windpipe
The singe on my pajama hem

A butterfly kiss on a stormy night
The pitter patter of raindrops on my windowsill

A Beauty Queen trapped inside a never-ending hallway
The sound of high heels click-clacking on the hardwood floor
Back and forth

The broken record skipping over grooves
The time warp
The stuck in the past

The wink
The curtsy
The ribbons and bows

## DREAMING

I fell off streets
Onto cliffs
Where oceans lie below
And cul-de-sacs lead to
Dead-ended answers to questions
Beckoning more

# BAREFOOT

Acoustic guitars
Harmonicas
Smooth voices singing stories speaking longing
Over my mother's car radio
Driving past The Troubador,
I'm not legal age
I can't go hear Ronee Blakely sing *Lightning Over Water*
Mom drives the winding canyon road
The Topanga Corral
Kris Kristofferson
Moonshine

Warm tone cinematography
*McCabe and Mrs. Miller*
Madness
*Apocalypse Now*
Wide open spaces
*Days of Heaven*
Is there an escape from cruelty?
*Deliverance*

Julie Christie
Robert Altman
Ned Beatty
John Boorman
Brooke Adams
Terrence Malick
Richard Gere
Bring me here
Hare Krishna Hare Krishna

Under tents on Ocean Park
Tambourines

Don't Eat Meat
Goat Farm
Carrot picking
Llamas
My brother lives in a cabin at the end of the canyon dirt road
Once upon a time ago Hazel Scott played the piano and sang him songs
Now he smokes
Hashish

Burl Ives gave my other brother his first guitar

Harem Pants
Braless
Sun stroked skin
Golden hair
Lemon
Succulent Peaches
Wet Sand under fingernails
Freshly painted toes
Freckles
Bloodshot eyes
Seaweed necklaces
Salt air
Sandstorms mudslides high tide
Sandstone seventies Topanga Canyon free love mom
Sandalwood
Earthworms
Driftwood
Fog

Open roads
Speeding cars

Canyon falls

Coyotes

School buses made into houses
Frogs
Pebbles stuck between toes
Men with sand-speckled beards
Teenagers with surfboards
The absence of school bells ringing
White wash spritzers
Pelican sunsets
Endless tomorrows
Sweeping sand with my toes
Til the tide comes knee high
And washes me away

## LIVING ON A THRU-WAY

This three hundred square foot living room with cottage
cheese ceilings and a gold brocade couch propped against
a window that was never designed to open stares out onto
a street that serves as the thru-way between one major
boulevard and the next
An Avenue meant for traveling through
Not to be the destination.
This low-hung stucco entrapment is pressing against my
chest
I'm lying flat on the floor counting curdles as though
they're sheep.
Life is emotional paralysis.
The cars are whizzing past neglecting the stop sign.
When the horns blare I shake my leg I bug out my eyes
I repeat out loud, "I've got to get up. I've got to get out."

## WEDDING DRESSES

I've never been inside a bridal shop, never worn white satin shoes
Petticoats or something borrowed something blue
My skin has never been white satin
Nor have my trains of glory trailed marble floors
Unless you count the time I spilled his coke between the cracks in his foyer
His mother caught me on all fours
Pity, she said, that you're a whore

*Karen Time*

## YOU'LL NEVER GET OVER IT

That word sticks with you – whore
You can never quite get over it
Even forty-one years later
The way his mother said it
Sitting at the kitchen table while I waited by the door
I already knew I wasn't good enough to set foot in their house
Let alone be her son's date to the prom
All the other high school girls
With their curls, cars and flawless complexions
Erased their transgressions with daddy's credit card
Privilege begets a purity
I never had the chance to know

## VIOLET ZIPPER SPANDEX

Who's that Rod Stewart knock-off in bed with me?
The sun has ripped the sky
And there are three new holes in my
Black tights
On the beige shag carpet
1979
My father died
I don't know where I am
She was just seventeen
My head is split in two
I have a boyfriend in Beverly Hills
Who looks like Joe Jackson
Got his wisdom teeth pulled
Yesterday afternoon
Last night I took the Santa Monica bus to Doheny
Walked up the hill ordered
A martini
I need Close-Up
Red gel
Please make the sun go down
Somewhere in Glendale
The Galleria
I used to shop there
Before violet zippered spandex
A Marlboro would do me good
My hands are shaking
He drives a Pacer
Have they caught the Hillside Strangler yet?

*Katie Legs*

## WHEN THE MUSIC'S LOUD

The music's loud and I can't hear what I smell
The house is burning behind the oven door

I run out of breath into hollow space
The chocolate shell of last year's Easter bunny
Sits half-wrapped in the butter drawer
The refrigerator is cold

I am not the one you love
I am not the holy saint
I am not sweet to taste
I am not soft to touch

I am the blankness in the darkest space

## SEE-THROUGH GLARE

I was standing on a bright and perky corner
Light bearing down and through my gauzy black dress
My thick purple tights melting bone
Last night's tequila bottle pounding the side of my head
Its worm pushing up out of ground
Seeking
When came dirt flecked reflection
Stage
Leather chaps a man heavy eyeliner singing
Then…Static
Four white walls with filled-out applications pinned to
Sunglassed man pins mine to wall
I stamp the worm down
Dive deep underground
I go back to that stage
To bouncing
To banging
To fast loud pulsation
To fury to chaos to banging of drums chopped up chords seething rhythms
To no more bright and perky or prom or graduation or friends going to college
I stood on a Sunset Strip corner
The blistering sun of a new day burning
A reckoning through my pores
I was not going to shine or make my mother proud or have the same friends I had yesterday

## THE IN-BETWEEN

Traveling out of sundrenched days
Into the stark black hallway
Permeating roads not alive or dead
The stagnant holding
Holding hands stagnation
The stagnant holding cell
Of the wait
For the light that is cast out
Of the thoughts
Holding me prisoner
I reach toward the others
Floating through the dark
We float
Entwined
Through our darkest hours
We can't remember laughter
Or the natural color of our hair
We poke abscesses with safety pins
Think back on Spin-the-Bottle
That first tongue that spun us full throttle to lust
Digging needles in
Pills down
Guzzling fire-breathing whiskey
Scorched lips
We are all the beauties gone patchy gray skin
Sitting on the edges of our mattresses
Hungry for meat and red wine
The savory sunburnt sky

## MEMORY FLASH

He nods out in the middle of a kiss
Skateboards past the Cathay de Grande
The night Christian Death plays
We watch Medea shoot Frankie up his first time fourteen years old
A transient Hollywood Boulevard hotel

I saw two junkies on the street yesterday one carrying a very large guitar case
veins popping out of his bones stringy overgrown shag in face heading down
First Avenue to the Lower East Side they all head down
Heroin's so cool

Carlton died he was twenty pounds the last time I saw him we were on Melrose he
needed ten dollars and a ride downtown
They all head down
Daphne overdosed she used to have shoes
This is on a loop on a loop on a loop: She had shoes when I didn't
She worked at Fred Segal I was eating condiments off taco stands and
panhandling She was better than me She was found dead on Errol Flynn's estate

Even after I gave up on dying I hung around the dead
Now on sunny days the junkies make my skin crawl
Yesterday I saw one on First Avenue making the sign of the cross
I wondered what deal he was making with God

On Sunday mornings when I'm on my way to work I pass a theater where a
church service is about to start
It is in the theater where once they showed films of my father's and where SICK OF IT ALL played a hardcore set the other night
Sundays a group of young hipster born agains are inside while outside six pasty bloated
men are looking for God between their knees
Once my father made a film about Jesus. It moves too slow a pace for me.
He stuck needles in his veins
Not Jesus
My father

## LOVE TRAP

Yesterday's danger in the shape of tonight's lover
The shadow stalker
Terrible how I relish his teeth on my neck

*Tippi Hedren*

## CARRIE SNODGRESS'S SWIMMING POOL

She's the mad housewife from the diary I've never seen before
Did she win an Academy Award?

She's fragile wired eyes lips that never need polish
She floats above water next to me
I've come to naked in her pool

Was on a thirty-day vacation from Thunderbird wine
Celebrated my return with a pint of 151
I was standing in Carrie Snodgress's kitchen toasting the disintegration of my sober mind
She was clapping taking my hand
Then

A wave of chlorinated water brushes my third belly roll
I was never this fat before

Her English boyfriend dog paddles closer
Later he will take me for a fast ride
Cranking the Damned's "Smash it Up"
I am in the backseat
Highland or Vine?

Her English boyfriend dog paddles to me
She is laughing smoke rings blowing over our heads
"Go ahead. Kiss him. If you like him it's all right."
No isn't in my vocabulary tonight
It's yes yes yes
Yes to liquor
Yes to coke
Yes to another woman's man

## NOTES ON SIDE STREETS

He tore the insides of the piano out
Turned it into a harp
He rode his skateboard home to Mt. Washington
Home to make music home to make music
His tattooed pierced body strung out

## BELONGING

The teenaged girl loud mouth drunk torn stockings living in squalor gets sober. Her mind keeps words under lock and key. She meets the boy colors her eyelids truck-stop blue her hair platinum her skull tattoo. I've been living with a bathroom door painted syringe blood stained best friend razor blade. These thoughts she'd like to express to the boy she loves who loves her not he only loves the drugs he shoots. They live together by the beach his syringes hidden behind the 12-Step books she forgets to read.

*Drinks to the Party*

## ISOLATED GIRL

Germs cassette tape, diary and pen, the kitchen table with wicker legs, the dying tree in the gray yard, the bed wet from his sweat the jones between the night and morning fix, my tear on page. I light another cigarette, pause between words in search of self nothing to grab but a blur.

*Pall Mall Break*

## IF YOU KNOW WHAT'S GOOD FOR YOU

Coming home with me will keep you out of heaven
Or late for your next Narcotics Anonymous meeting
His works are on the coffee table
I'll bring you milk and sugar
Even though I know you want the spoon
The Book of Matches
I heard you qualifying
I had identification
You were going to be my first best friend without drugs
But I brought you home
The needle and the balloon
The dirty cotton
They were all waiting for you

*Party Girl*

*Super Nipple*

## FRANKLIN AVENUE

Dark haired beauty leaves me stranded on a corner. Cars of different colors and sizes race through the yellow lights to make it to the other side. This avenue leads to the Shakespeare Bridge to the nightlife to the boulevard of stars the hills where I grew up.

How could she leave me here with no way out? How can a block of cement turn to quicksand chain my feet to yesterday?

Western curves to Los Feliz the entrance to Ferndell Park magical stone fishponds built in grass. As a child I watched the guppies swim searching for the sea. As a child I ran from my stepbrother who took me hiking on a back trail pulled his pants down ordered me touch. I kicked running not knowing my destination. I was the guppy searching for the ocean landed on this very corner where I wait for the dark hair beauty and shrink back to then.

Where do you go when you're a child and your house is unsafe and you don't want to go to the Astro Burger because you've seen what happens to the runaways who end up there on those Made-For-TV-Movies and you're only ten too young for pimps? You go home again and hope he doesn't step through your bedroom door tonight.

How could she simply say I can't come get you when she's run these streets herself when she slept on my floor a cracked-out whore. How could she leave me with no place to go?

## HUNGRY

I wait for you to call like a hungry dog waiting at the door wanting food I don't know why I'm lonely I have you I have so much love I don't see you every night I see you in the morning when you are asleep and when you come home after midnight I jump up out of bed and run to the front door like a little girl who's been waiting ten years for her father to come home.

## BACK FLAT DOWN

I was on the back back of his Vespa
Riding to the movies
My hand on his hip
Whispering into his ear
A promise, that this date was going to return us
To that tongue twister night of our first encounter
When language came to me in the form of body
When I spoke with a thrust of the hip
My back flat
Down

In the beginning we went to the movies
We snuck into the women's bathroom during the screening of *Parasite**
I let him feel me up during *Swamp Thing*
But by *Cat People* I'd gotten it into my head I wanted to be a good girl
I wouldn't let him slip his hand inside my panties

I didn't mean to chase him into another girl's bed

How could I expect him to want me?
I was shrieking silence
I was the glass ashtray flying across the living room

All I wanted was to be good
But, really, what good is a girl when speech escapes her?
What good is a girl who loses sexuality?
What good is a girl when that girl is me?

Self-loathing loathing self

Loathing becomes the lather with which I wash myself

He came home unexpectantly
Caught me
In the middle of a prayer
Begging for restoration
He took me in his arms
Apologized for his infidelity
For his expectations
For not seeing
How torn up inside I was

I was on the back back of his Vespa
No helmut wall or chain
My windswept eyelashes bracing against speed
We were only a boulevard's length away from our
revitalization
When he said, "Oh shit, a car."
And the ton of steel hit our wheel
I rocketed up into the sky
Shot down back flat on pavement unguarded head crash
Back flat
Down

*Not the Academy Award winning movie, *Parasite*, the 3-D movie, *Parasite*, starring Demi Moore.

## THREE DAY COMA

I'm a body on a bed in a room off a hallway where felons march single file their legs in chains clanking like the elephants chained to the parking lot fence across the street from the Hollywood Bowl the night *The Decline of Western Civilization* opened on the Boulevard and the riot squad stood in waiting with their gear and the helicopters overhead made us run for cover. We found shelter underneath a former homeless encampment. Bushes made out of beer bottles. The crunch of glass under steel toe boots. Shhhhhhh. The riot squad will find us and beat us black and blue. I'm a body on a bed. My face is a scab. We escaped the riot squad. They never got their hands on me. The felons march further down the hallway their chains a clink a clink clinking. I'm a body on a bed.

## DO YOU SEE ME, LIKE I SAW YOU?

I could see the crash playing between the play and twinkle
of her glamour day stories
Every time she caught me staring, she turned away
Afraid my stare would push crashing memories to the
forefront

All I can remember are the words, "Oh shit a car!"
All I feel is the numbness in my knee
All I want is a scab-free face
A mirror with a princess reflection

Her Hollywood stories make me squirm
They end badly
They end without him
They end in a car crash on Doheny Drive

She was trailblazing, or maybe just blazing, in Topanga
Canyon
When the ambulance delivered me to downtown L.A.'s
emergency room
No phones atop the Santa Monica mountains
No access to mothers
Rolling down the grassy slopes arm in arm with whoever
lover

I'm lying on a cot in the hallway outside of the X-ray room
When the doctors finally reach her
She was alone in Cedars-Sinai
Without a mother to run to her rescue
How was she supposed to know I was in trouble?

I never called her with my problems
I simply wore them on my face
I never told her he was a junkie
She never told me my father was
Not that he was responsible for her car crash

There are all sorts of crashes

*Titty Tweakin'*

## REBIRTH

I am the streak of light streaming through the crack
The sea splash
The frolic
Bare toes skimming the mist dripped grass
The sprinkles on your ice cream cone
Your first sand pail
The yellow teddy bear your father gave you
Your first A
Your mother's laughter
Your grandmother's hug
Your big sister's inclusion
Sensations of being awestruck
*Cabaret*, Liza Minnelli
*Lady Sings the Blues*, Diana Ross
Linda Ronstadt, David Bowie
Robert Louis Stevenson
Curious George
Christmas lights on Hollywood Boulevard
Barbra Streisand in *Funny Girl*
Nancy Drew
Wonder
Best friend
The deserts star-drenched sky
Cactus
Motorcycle races
The revving of engines
Dirt in your faces
Under your fingernails
In between your teeth
The engines
The revving

The winner breaking through the finish line
The cheers
The happier memories once in shadow breaking through
Beaming
Calling you out from under
An invitation from the eternal friend
A hand
A reaching
An embrace

*Hider and Seeker*

## SHE

She scoops pralines and cream
At the Baskin Robbins
Western Avenue——————————-Hollywood
She walks through the hills
Dried milky patches across wrists
Digs secrets into staircases
Thirty years passing
All the way home

## LOS ANGELES in FLASHBACK

An overcast Spring afternoon. Dewy, leather jacket, dirty gel hair. Riding home after watching *At Close Range*. Christopher Walken. Sean Penn. Father and son. Crime-wave, bloody, betrayal. My father's friend's son wrote the screenplay and I wonder. Madonna sings the theme song. I want to sit next to the Mulholland Fountain where my high school friends and I gathered on weekend nights. Staring at Marilyn Monroe's footprints in the cement of Grauman's Chinese Theater after the movie thinking of *The Misfits* and wanting to be a needle in my vein. Heading east on Hollywood Boulevard passing Vine hanging a right on Gower stopping. I'm having a nicotine fit. Walking into the liquor store to buy a pack of cigarettes a man racing by me. I'm following the red dots. Was that a gun? The store clerk is pushing me out into the street. The robbery was a continuation of the movie. Reality and fiction always blur and past and present bare no distinction. I'm back on the back of my new boyfriend's motorcycle (not the Vespa: not that boyfriend). Gower Gulch. Late night eggs at Denny's watching the Scientology busses passing through the night. I'm waiting for something to be different, but it is always the same. There are no palm trees on the street where I live. Just another Denny's and a freeway off ramp. They smoke crack in the laundry room and breed roaches in apartment number two. I live here because the rent is cheap and I can afford to buy new clothes every week. Changing changing driving driving Hollywood to Sunset Sunset to paradise screech. Passing Ballard Hardware on Hyperion I'm ten again wandering inside the store because I live a few blocks away, no other reason. I have no need for hammer and nails. Thirty years after the liquor store heist, my friends stop at the store, Wacko, and my mind is racing around the history of this building. First there was the Post Office and then there was the stationary store, Nasons, where I spent Sunday afternoons after church loading up on watermelon scented erasers, or, was Nasons first and then the Post Office? Think. Think. The friends I'm with weren't here when Wacko was the Soap Plant or when Soap Plant was a small store east on Sunset that sold, you guessed it, soap. My childhood best friend and I walk from Ballard Hardware to the Soap Plant, just for something to do, and one day, in addition to soap, the Soap Plant starts selling used Levis and my best friend steals a pair without anyone knowing, myself included. One year later she is arrested for burglary and I am arrested for drugs, handcuffed on Talmadge Avenue, the avenue named after the Talmadge Sisters, silent film stars who never made it into the talkies. Talking is overrated anyway. I'd much rather watch the scenery pass by.

*Liquor Glass*

## GHOSTS

I'm a sinking ship
Far away from Treasure Island
Inside a house where gusts of wind blow cold
And the creaking of its old bones
Turn to a Hyena's bark
Waking me long after
The moon takes full bloom
I'm face to face with shadows
I'm a scream without sound
A muzzle without mouth
A breath without lungs
I'm running from childhood ghosts
A sea captain without a steer
Holding rot iron railings
Slipping barefoot
Down down down
The hard stone staircases
Breathlessly, silently
Slipping through the cracks in the darkness where the light
shines through

## LIFETIMES

You are a lifetime ago
When I burned rice
Lived on Cup of Soup
Paced the hardwood floors
In need of
Sugar
Vitamin B-12
A happy memory
A phone call
A voicemail
Your voice
An apology
Your undying love
Realistic dreams
Pragmatism
Baptism
A plane ticket
A new world

*Model Break*

## DAY DEW DREAM OF A GIRL IN HER SNOW GLOBE WORLD

I thought I thought I thought I could dream my way out
from behind the glass
Into into into the boulevards where glitter falls from the sky
where pockmarked roads masquerade as crystal balls
and the future holds you out for me
to run into your arms
to feel your breath on my neck
to realize I've been saved.

Falling falling falling falling
Falling from the sky

I press my lips on the glass a window to tumble through
My breath rap rap rapping
Come to me come to me come to me
I'm dying

The dome was so small
A miniature world
I could easily inhabit
I thought thought thought
Until the moisture was sucked out
The heat began to rise
And no matter how hard I tried
I couldn't breathe.

Gasping grasping I mean I'm gasping I'm aghast I mean
I'm grasping I mean I'm reaching
You are falling from the sky a million tiny stars

You are the somersault internal eternal eternally
disrupting calm
I crawl to you to the border to the edge to the periphery to
the sea to the globe to the moon
My knees are scraped my hands are blistered my feet
swollen my tongue bleeding
I am spilling out into the streets a running disaster not fit
for life or love a gurgling newborn awaiting
transformation when I see a shape in the distance and a cool
breeze breathes down on this fever and the snow
begins to fall
Falling falling falling

You are the fallen snow the salve the sprinkle of heaven the
one who lets the moisture in the key the key the key the key
the key the key

To the boulevards

****

cast away the nights of yore and find the love that brings
me forth

****

*One Drink In*

## CREAK of the FLOORBOARD

I should hate men
After what you did
When I was 8,9,10,11
Sneaking into my room
After our parents fell asleep.
The creaking floorboards
Were the warning bell you were coming
To wreak havoc on my body
To wreak havoc on my mind
Wreaking havoc on my future
You were the wrecking ball crucifying my identity.
I should fear men
Because of you.
Yet, they know not what you did
They listen to my held breath
Cooing in my ear
Harder baby harder
Softer baby softer
Silent goes the night.
Decades older
I lie here in repose
Thinking back on what you stole
My right to say no
Those evenings of degradation and coming to
The end of me
I should be dead.
I inhale let my living sink in.

You aren't the winner here
You're not my captor
You aren't my forever.
What you did won't make me hate
A man
Who never makes the floorboard creak.

You are not every man
And every man is not you.
You no longer decide the fate of me
You no longer possess my identity.
The he who is not you whispers in my ear, "I will always keep you safe."
The he who is the antithesis of you
Makes the floorboard stop creaking
Takes the fear out of night
Removes hatred from my heart

## LOVE POEM #1

My dress
Lifts up over
And under the pillow
Cases falling onto the floor
Spread out

My arms
His hands firmly
Press against the cotton
Sheets the bedsprings squeak
Love makes me
So shy

*Two Drinks In*

## FLIGHT

If I could part ways with my flesh would I be free of those
memories that trick me into hating my body?

If I were weightless could I lift off pavement be a rocket to
the moon?

If I was a space suit could I float away be a balloon
escaping into the sky no one able to reach my string?

If I could reassemble myself attach my left leg where my
right arm oughta be would I land inside a Picasso?

If I were hanging off a screw drilled into a pristine gallery
wall would I take comfort in being stared at?

If you hadn't touched me would I have lived my life
thinking every stranger saw the dirt on my face?

If I had been alive in 1938 would I have been cast in
*Angels with Dirty Faces?*

If I was a Fragonard cherub would joy be my bounty?

If I was joyful would his trespasses leave my thoughts
alone?

## STAY

I know you
        Move your hand
Away from my thigh
My heart, my body, me
I love you
I know you
        Go away
Stay here
I'm panicked
        Bring your hand
Closer
Your fingers
Near
Your ear to my heart beating rapidly
Running away
Running toward
Running in place
        Running to stay

*Dance Party*

*Flasher in the Park*

## DARLING…I

Darling?
Yes, mother?
Darling?
Yes?
Darl?
Yes?
I'm sorry I never stopped him from
I'm sorry I never said I was sorry
I'm sorry I left you alone in the hospital
I'm sorry I married your stepfather
I'm sorry I wasn't a good mother
I'm sorry
For your promiscuity?
For not knowing how to say no?
For having been on your own at too young an age?
For making sure…
Darling? My mother
Your mother?
My mother married a man just like your father
It was your mother's fault?
Life is nobody's fault
I'm sorry I lashed out at you
I'm sorry I needed you to fix it
I'm sorry I didn't see everything you were doing for us
I'm sorry
For my free spirit?
You always put what you needed in front of what I needed
I wasn't meant to parent
I know
Doesn't mean I loved you any less than a mother who was born to nurture

Mother?
Darling?
Yes, mother?
Darling, I…
I…

*Garden Party*

## WAKE UP

You were having a bad dream
I was having a bad dream
What were you dreaming?
I was dreaming
You were screaming
I was screaming at him to stop
In your dream
In my dream
He comes at me when I'm sleeping
That was a long time ago
A long time ago

# More Crime Fiction by CHRIS D.

Half-sisters, schoolteacher Mona and junkie punk rocker Terri, are uneasy roommates while taking care of their sick mother. When their boyfriends, cop Johnny Cullen and killer Merle Chambers, clash due to labor struggles in their small town of Devil's River, the two women are pulled into the fray. To make matters worse, jealous female sheriff, Billie Travers, decides Mona is intruding on her faltering love affair, and quiet small town life amps up into an apocalyptic nightmare of uncontrollable violence and destruction.

Corrupt female police detective, Frankie Powers, is treading water in her small desert hometown of Sweet Home, California. Burned-out and emotionally numb after losing her husband and child in a mysterious fire ten years before, her conscience is reawakened when her affair with a Bakersfield narc brings new facts to light. Frankie's mob boss uncle, Jack Richman, has been kidnapping underage girls for his Vegas prostitution syndicate; he's also been victimizing his own teen daughters, Frankie's twin bad girl cousins, Valerie and Vanessa. Soon Frankie finds herself singlehandedly fighting tooth-and-nail against not only wicked uncle Jack but also his dominatrix wife, Marilyn and their degenerate hitman, Cal Nero. Can a lone shewolf survive against the bloodthirsty pack?

# AVAILABLE NOW

## FROM POISON FANG BOOKS

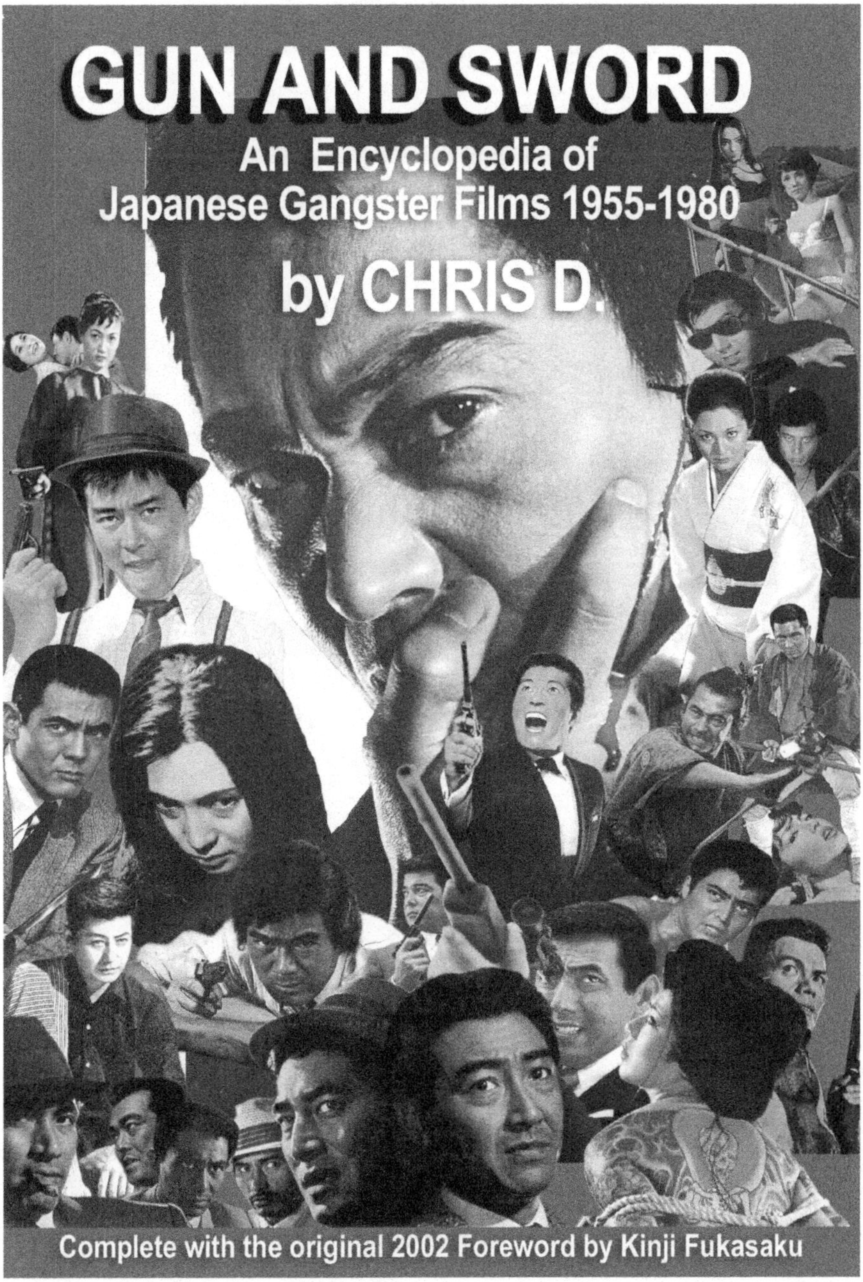

Made in the USA
Columbia, SC
10 July 2023

20038036R00057